WELCOME TO MY COUNTRY

Welcome to
COLOMBIA

Gareth Stevens Publishing
A WORLD ALMANAC EDUCATION GROUP COMPANY

Written by
LIM BEE HONG/LESLIE JERMYN

Designed by
LYNN CHIN

Picture research by
SUSAN JANE MANUEL

First published in North America in 2000 by
Gareth Stevens Publishing
A World Almanac Education Group Company
1555 North RiverCenter Drive, Suite 201
Milwaukee, Wisconsin 53212 USA

For a free color catalog describing
Gareth Stevens' list of high-quality books
and multimedia programs, call
1-800-542-2595 (USA) or
1-800-461-9120 (CANADA).
Gareth Stevens Publishing's
Fax: (414) 225-0377.

© **TIMES MEDIA PRIVATE LIMITED 2000**
Originated and designed by
Times Editions
An imprint of Times Media Private Limited
Times Centre, 1 New Industrial Road
Singapore 536196
http://www.timesone.com.sg/te

Library of Congress Cataloging-in-Publication Data

Lim Bee Hong.
Welcome to Colombia / Lim Bee Hong and Leslie Jermyn.
p. cm. — (Welcome to my country)
Includes bibliographical references and index.
Summary: An overview of the history, geography, government,
economy, people, and culture of Colombia.
ISBN 0-8368-2508-X (lib. bdg.)
1. Colombia—Juvenile literature. [1. Colombia.]
I. Jermyn, Leslie. II. Title. III. Series.
F2258.5.L56   2000
986.1—dc21   00-020206

Printed in Malaysia

1 2 3 4 5 6 7 8 9 04 03 02 01 00

PICTURE CREDITS
Archive Photos: 35, 36
Victor Englebert: 1, 3 (bottom), 7, 8, 9 (top), 11
  (top), 17, 19, 23 (bottom), 25, 26, 27, 28, 30,
  31, 34, 37, 45
Eduardo Gil: 3 (center), 18, 23 (top), 40
The Hutchison Library: 3 (top), 5, 6, 9
  (bottom), 16, 20, 21 (both), 32 (top), 33,
  38, 41
Klingwall: 12 (bottom)
North Wind Picture Archives: 12 (top)
Chip and Rosa Maria Peterson: 2, 4, 10, 11
  (bottom), 13, 15 (both), 22, 24, 32 (bottom)
South American Pictures: Cover, 29, 39
Lesley Thelander: 14
Topham Picturepoint: 43

Digital Scanning by Superskill Graphics Pte Ltd

Contents

5 **Welcome to Colombia!**

6 **The Land**

10 **History**

16 **Government and the Economy**

20 **People and Lifestyle**

28 **Language**

30 **Arts**

34 **Leisure**

40 **Food**

42 **Map**

44 **Quick Facts**

46 **Glossary**

47 **Books, Videos, Web Sites**

48 **Index**

Words that appear in the glossary are printed in **boldface** type the first time they occur in the text.

Welcome to Colombia!

Colombia is named after Christopher Columbus, who arrived in the Americas in the fifteenth century. The fourth largest country in South America, Colombia is home to four hundred Indian tribes. Let's explore Colombia, its friendly inhabitants, and its varied flora and fauna.

Opposite: Cycling is very popular in Colombia. Many people attend cycling races, both as competitors and as spectators.

Below: Buses, called *chivas* (CHEE-vahs), are common on Colombian roads.

The Flag of Colombia

The current Colombian flag was adopted in 1861. The top yellow band represents the nation of Colombia. The center blue band represents the sea that separates Colombia from Spain. The bottom red band represents independence and the blood shed in the process of gaining independence.

The Land

Located in the northwestern corner of South America, Colombia has a land area of 440,831 square miles (1,141,752 square kilometers). The Colombian territory includes islands in the Pacific Ocean and the Caribbean Sea, such as Malpelo and San Andrés. The capital of Colombia is Bogotá.

Regions

Colombia is divided into four distinct regions separated by mountain ranges. They are the Andean highlands, the Caribbean lowlands, the Pacific

Below: The highest peak in Colombia is Cristóbal Colón. It stands at 18,947 feet (5,775 meters) and is part of the Sierra Nevada de Santa Marta.

lowlands, and the Eastern plains. About 40 percent of the population lives in the fertile river valleys of the Andean highlands. The capital of Bogotá and the Magdalena River, the most important river in Colombia, are located in this region.

Cartagena, Barranquilla, and Santa Marta are major ports on the coast of the Caribbean lowlands. The sparsely inhabited Eastern plains occupy about 60 percent of the country's land area.

Above: Rain forests receive a lot of rain every year.

Climate

Colombia is located near the **equator**, and temperatures do not vary greatly between seasons. The country has two wet and two dry seasons. Climate is determined by **altitude**, and it gets colder the higher you go. "Hot country" refers to the coastal lowland areas, "**temperate** country" includes the valleys and basins in the Andean region, and "cold country" includes mountain areas above 912 feet (278 m).

Plants and Animals

Colombia's varied terrain has enabled many types of plants to thrive in it. About 15 percent of all plant species can be found in Colombia. Many species are found only in Colombia.

Animals found in Colombia include 358 species of mammals, such as wild cats and bears; 15 percent of all living primates; and 1,700 species of birds, such as eagles, hummingbirds, and gulls.

Above: Scarlet macaws, with their bright plumes, are easy to spot in the Amazon rain forest.

Left: Yellow highland flowers are one of the many plant species that thrive in Colombia.

History

Early Settlers and the Spaniards

Indigenous peoples inhabited Colombia before the Spaniards arrived. Their numbers declined after the Spanish conquest.

In 1536, Spaniard Gonzalo Jiménez de Quesada led an expedition inland. The Spaniards defeated the Chibchas, the largest Indian tribe at the time. With the support of Spain's King Charles, Quesada laid claim to the land.

Bogotá was founded in 1538. In 1549, it was made the administrative center of New Granada. In 1718, New Granada included Colombia, Panama, Ecuador, and Venezuela.

Above: A model of Christopher Columbus's ship, the *Santa María,* is displayed at the Museo Nacional in the Colombian capital of Bogotá.

The Fight for Independence

By the end of the eighteenth century, the people in Colombia started to crave independence. Simón Bolívar led the resistance against Spain in New Granada. Bolívar wanted the union of

Left: The Monument to Independence was erected on the site where Simón Bolívar defeated the Spanish forces in 1819.

all Spanish-speaking countries in South America but received no cooperation from the other leaders.

From 1815 to 1817, a Spanish force, led by General Pablo Morillo, killed many people in Colombia who were suspected of supporting independence. From 1818 to 1821, Bolívar and Francisco de Paula Santander fought the Spaniards and succeeded in regaining control over the whole country. By 1826, all the Spanish colonies in South America had become independent.

Below: In 1815, General Pablo Morillo led a Spanish force to reestablish control over Colombia.

Gran Colombia

Gran Colombia, established by Bolívar in the 1821 constitution, united Colombia, Ecuador, Venezuela, and Panama. When Bolívar died in 1830, the union dissolved.

Conservatives versus Liberals

Two parties emerged in the new nation — the **conservatives** and **liberals**. From 1899 to 1903, many Colombians died in the War of a Thousand Days, a civil war between the two parties. This war

Left: In 1953, in the midst of extreme chaos and violence, Gustavo Rojas Pinilla took control of the government.

weakened Colombia and enabled the United States to gain control of Panama.

Opposite, below: A statue of Simon Bolívar stands in the center of the Plaza de Bolívar in Bogotá.

From 1948 to 1958, Colombia went through a chaotic and brutal period known as The Violence. In 1953, Gustavo Rojas Pinilla, the commander of the army, took control of the government. In 1958, the two parties formed a **coalition**, called the National Front, to end Pinilla's **dictatorship**. The coalition lasted until 1974, when new elections were held.

Violence and the Drug Wars

In the 1970s and 1980s, the two political parties of the coalition **repressed** people who opposed them. This led to the formation of **guerilla** groups to fight the government. The Drug Wars also occurred at this time, when drug gangs organized squads to kill government officials who opposed them. The violence caused by guerilla groups and drug lords continued until the 1990s. Today, the government has had some success in controlling the situation.

Below: The Violence, or *La Violencia* (lah vee-oh-LAYN-see-ah), was the worst period in Colombian history. From 1948 to 1958, supporters of the two political parties battled in the streets and the countryside.

Gonzalo Jiménez de Quesada (1495–1579)

Born in Spain, Quesada led an expedition into Colombia in 1536 and established the area of New Granada. In old age, Quesada led another expedition to Colombia. The expedition failed, and Quesada died of leprosy in the Cordillera Central.

Gonzalo Jiménez de Quesada

Francisco de Paula Santander (1792–1840)

In 1821, Santander became the vice-president of Gran Colombia. After the union was dissolved in 1830, Santander became the first elected president of New Granada (Colombia).

Francisco de Paula Santander

Jorge Eliécer Gaitán (1902–1948)

A major member of the Liberal Party and a presidential candidate, Gaitán was assassinated in 1948. Because he was supported by the common people, his death caused huge riots in Bogotá.

Government and the Economy

The 1886 constitution gave a lot of power to the president and very little to Congress and the judiciary. In the late 1980s, the people became dissatisfied with this constitution. In May 1990, the people voted for the formation of a special assembly to establish a new constitution. On July 4, 1991, a new constitution was established.

Below: Guards stand in front of the Government Palace in Bogotá.

Legislative power lies with Congress, which has two houses — the Senate, with 102 members elected nationally, and the Chamber of Deputies, with members elected by each department, or state.

The Supreme Court controls justice in the country. There are sixty-one judicial districts. Below the national government are the department and city levels of government.

Above: Elections in Colombia are lively events. In 1954, women obtained the right to vote.

Economy

Colombia's main trading partners include the United States, Germany, and other Latin American countries. The country's main exports are cotton, coal, oil, coffee, bananas, textiles, and cut flowers.

Above: Freshly cut flowers are major export products.

Natural Resources

Agriculture and forestry are important to Colombia's economy. Coffee is one of the main crops. With half the country covered by forests, lumber and paper products are also important.

The mining and energy industries make up 40 percent of foreign trade. The main products include platinum, oil, coal, silver, iron ore, limestone, zinc, copper, and gold. About 90 percent of the world's emeralds are found in Colombia.

Industry

Many manufactured goods are produced for the country's local market. Big industries include chemicals, textiles, and food. Tourism is also a major industry in Colombia.

Above: Iron ore mined by workers is turned into powder.

People and Lifestyle

The Colombian population is divided into many groups distinguished by geographic and social differences. Attitudes toward family and religion, however, are similar in all groups.

Three economic classes exist in Colombia — the poor, the rich, and the middle class. About half the population is poor. The rich own land and businesses. Between these two extremes is the middle class, made up of professionals.

Below: One of the most traditional Indian groups in Colombia, the Guambiano Indians, lives in the town of Silvia.

Left: These girls represent some of the ethnic groups in Colombia. Mestizos make up about 8 percent of the population, whites and mulattoes about 3 percent each, Afro-Colombians about 5 percent, and Indians 1 percent.

Ethnic groups include mestizos (of Indian and white descent), whites (of Spanish descent), mulattoes (of white and black descent), Afro-Colombians (of African descent), and Indians. The largest ethnic group is the criollos, who are of white and mestizo descent.

Above: Most Afro-Colombians live in the Chocó department.

In Colombia, whites are generally better educated and earn a larger income than people of mixed descent. Historically, Afro-Colombians and Indians worked as laborers on farms owned by white Spaniards. Today, more opportunities are available.

Family Matters

Family ties are very strong in Colombia, and children usually remain close to their parents throughout their lives.

Traditionally, in the middle- and upper middle-class families, the man was the head of the household, and the woman stayed home to look after the children and the house. Women from poorer families were required to work

Above: On weekends, many Colombians enjoy spending time with their families at public parks.

to support the family. Today, more and more women from all classes are being educated and joining the workforce.

In a practice similar to godparenting, called *compadrazgo* (kohm-pah-DRAHZ-goh), friends of the family can become part of that family. Parents of a newborn may invite two friends or associates to become *compadres* (kohm-PAH-drays), or godparents, for the child. Compadres give the child financial and emotional support.

Above: A large, extended family sometimes lives together in the same house.

Left: This family is having fun making candy.

Education

Traditionally, only males from rich families were educated. Today, the government is trying to make education available to everyone, but schools in rural areas are still **inferior** to those in the cities. Even with an increase in government spending on education, there are still not enough schools, especially in rural areas.

Below: Well-to-do Colombian children attend schools with good facilities.

Left: Schools in rural areas are very basic and lack proper facilities. This school in a rain forest is actually a hut built on stilts. Although there is a shortage of schools in rural areas, the **literacy** rate in Colombia is 87 percent for those over fifteen years of age.

Since the 1980s, the government has tried to address the education problem by building more public schools and making education more affordable for the less **privileged**. Also, more women are going to college.

Health Care

Colombians living in the cities receive better health care than those in rural areas. Rural health facilities are poorly equipped, and public health care workers do not often visit these areas.

Religion

The majority of Colombians are Roman Catholic. The constitution of 1886 declared Roman Catholicism the official religion of Colombia. The church controlled many aspects of life, such as marriage and education.

In 1973, the government and the church signed an agreement that transferred control over health care, education, marriage, and other matters from the church to the government. Today, the Roman Catholic Church continues to exert a strong influence

Below: Life in the town of Cali centers around the Plaza de Caicedo, which is surrounded by the main cathedral and museums.

over the lives of the people. Priests are very important members of the community, and the church is the heart of every town.

Minority religious groups in Colombia include Jews and Protestants. Many Jews, however, moved to other countries, especially after the political violence of the 1980s. Protestant missionaries help people in rural areas.

Above: First Communion is one of the most important events in a Roman Catholic child's life.

Language

The official language of Colombia is Spanish, which was the language of the Spaniards who conquered Colombia and other countries in South America. The Spanish alphabet is similar to the English one, but it has three extra letters. Spanish can be easier to learn than English because the words are pronounced exactly as they are written. Spanish is the most widely spoken

Left:
Newsstands in Colombia sell local and international newspapers and magazines.

language in Colombia, but some of the indigenous peoples have kept their own languages. People from different regions and social classes speak different Spanish dialects.

Colombian literature has flourished since the days of independence. Today, many Colombian writings have been translated into English. One of the most famous Colombian writers is Gabriel García Márquez.

Arts

Early Influences

Colombian art has been influenced by Indian, Spanish, and African cultures. Before the arrival of the Spaniards, the indigenous peoples produced jewelry and sculptures, with unique styles for each tribe. After the Spanish conquest, painting, sculpture, and architecture were greatly influenced by Spanish culture. Spanish styles were dominant until the twentieth century.

Below: Colombians and tourists visit an art market in Cali.

The Twentieth Century

After World War II, many cities were modernized, and skyscrapers rose alongside colonial buildings. Since the 1930s, many great artists have flourished in Colombia. Three of the country's best known artists are Alejandro Obregón, Enrique Grau, and Fernando Botero. Botero's sculptures and paintings are displayed around the world. A unique feature of Botero's work is that his human and animal figures are always fat.

Above: This sculpture stands at the Santillana Center in Medellín.

Left: Music festivals in Colombia feature talented performers.

Music

Traditionally, indigenous peoples played many kinds of drums and flutes. Colombian music shows influences from many cultures, including African and Spanish. Two of the most popular forms of modern Colombian music are salsa from the Caribbean and tango from Argentina. Both salsa and tango music are accompanied by dance steps.

Above: Outside of school, privileged children also take singing, dancing, and music lessons.

Crafts

Colombians are very creative and use many materials to produce artistic crafts. Indigenous peoples weave baskets from the fibers of cactus, palms, agave, and bamboo. Fine cloth weaving is another traditional Colombian craft. The Mompós area is famous for its gold **filigree** jewelry. The Cuna Indians are noted for their *molas* (MOH-lahs), or decorative textile panels. The Antioquia area features quality leather products, such as shoulder bags.

Below: Many types of pottery can be purchased in Colombia.

Leisure

Chess

Chess is the most popular game in Colombia. It is enjoyed by young and old alike. Colombian chess players are the best in South America, and many are sent to the Chess Olympiads.

What Colombians Do for Fun

Many Colombians enjoy watching television, especially the *telenovela*

Below: Young children enjoy chess just as much as the adults do.

(tay-lay-noh-VAY-lah), a program similar to a soap opera that follows the life and times of a family.

Young people enjoy a *rumba* (ROOM-bah), a party where friends meet to eat, drink, and dance until late in the evening. People in the cities enjoy going to the movies. Large cities offer many cultural events, such as art exhibitions and concerts.

Many Colombian women take part in beauty pageants, which are seen as ways to gain fame and fortune.

Soccer Mania

Soccer is perhaps the most popular sport in Colombia. The national team has participated in many international competitions, such as the World Cup and the Pan-American Games.

Other Sports

Other popular sports in Colombia include baseball and basketball.

Left: Carlos Valderrama, the Colombian team captain in the 1998 World Cup finals, is known for his superb soccer skills and his outrageous hair.

The country has also done well in international competitions in cycling and boxing. Boxing events attract crowds of spectators. Boxers Kid Pambelé and Rodrigo Valdés have won many world competitions. The Spaniards introduced bullfighting to Colombia. The bullring in Bogotá brings in many fans.

Colombians also enjoy water sports, such as swimming, scuba diving, waterskiing, and snorkeling.

Above: Colombians head to the many beaches for the sun or just to relax with family and friends.

Holy Week and Corpus Christi

Holy Week starts a week before Easter, on Palm Sunday. The biggest celebrations occur in the city of Popayán, with a spectacular candlelight procession through the streets.

A Catholic festival, Corpus Christi is a celebration of the Eucharist, or Holy Communion. All across the country, people gather to construct elaborate altars out of simple materials, such as paper, flowers, and cloth.

Below: Holy Week processions are very colorful and bright events. People assemble along the streets to watch.

Christmas and Independence Day

People in the Cauca River Valley play "Shouted Christmas Presents." Two teams of people who are about the same size face each other. Members of each team wear identical costumes. The leaders of each team then try to identify each other without speaking.

Colombia celebrates Independence Day on July 20, with parades by military units and schoolchildren.

Above: During Christmas, schoolchildren in Colombia have fun making Santa Claus face masks and other decorations.

Food

Colombian Meals

Colombians have three meals a day. Breakfast is a small meal, accompanied by coffee. Lunch is the biggest meal of the day and often consists of a bowl of soup; a main dish of meat, fish, or poultry; and dessert. Dinner is usually small, consisting of a main dish and perhaps soup. People living in the highland areas eat mostly meat. Those living on the coasts eat mostly fish.

Below: In Colombia, live chickens can be purchased at the market.

Left: *Empanadas* (aym-pah-NAH-dahs), or pastries stuffed with meat and vegetables, are popular snacks sold in market stalls in Colombia.

Favorite Foods

Colombians enjoy grilled beef, stewed beef with sauce, chicken with rice, and grilled fish. The most popular food in Colombia is *arepas* (ah-REE-pahs), or cornbread. Around Bogotá, people enjoy *ajiaco santafereño* (ah-hee-AH-koh sahn-tah-fay-RAYN-yoh), a soup made from avocados, chicken, corn, and capers. For dessert, people enjoy fresh fruits and sweets made from milk.

CARIBBEAN SEA

Providencia

San Andrés

PANAMA

Santa Marta
Barranquilla
ATLÁNTICO
Cartagena

Cristóbal Colón
(18,947 ft / 5,775 m)

Sierra
Nevada de
Santa Marta

LA GUAJIRA

MAGDALENA

CÉSAR

SUCRE

CÓRDOBA

BOLÍVAR

**NORTE DE
SANTANDER**

VENEZUELA

Sinú

Magdalena

Atrato

Orinoco

ANTIOQUIA

Medellín

SANTANDER

CHOCÓ

CALDAS

RISARALDA

QUINDÍO

BOYACÁ

CUNDINAMARCA

BOGOTÁ

**PACIFIC
OCEAN**

Buenaventura

Cali

TOLIMA

**VALLE DEL
CAUCA**

CORDILLERA CENTRAL

Popayán

HUILA

META

CAUCA

NARIÑO

CAQUETÁ

Equator

BRAZIL

ECUADOR

PERU

Amazon

COLOMBIA

State Boundary

■ **Capital**

● **City**

River

N

Above: A quiet town in the Cauca department.

Amazon River D5
Antioquia B2
Atlántico B1
Atrato River A2

Barranquilla B1
Bogotá B3
Bolívar B2
Boyacá B3
Brazil D4
Buenaventura A3

Caldas B3
Cali B3
Caquetá B4
Caribbean Sea
   A1–B1
Cartagena B1
Cauca A3
César B1
Chocó A3

Cordillera Central B3
Córdoba B2
Cristóbal Colón B1
Cundinamarca B3

Ecuador A5

Huila B3

La Guajira C1

Magdalena B1
Magdalena River B2
Medellín B2
Meta C3

Nariño A4
Norte de Santander
   C2

Orinoco River D2

Pacific Ocean A3
Panama A1–A2
Peru B5
Popayán A3
Providencia A1

Quindío B3

Risaralda B3

San Andrés A1

Santa Marta B1
Santander B2
Sierra Nevada de
   Santa Marta B1
Sinú River B2
Sucre B1

Tolima B3

Valle del Cauca A3
Venezuela C2–D2

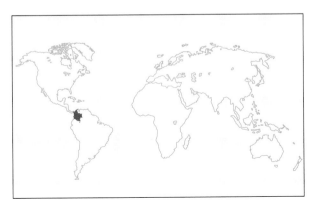

Quick Facts

Official Name	República de Colombia, Republic of Colombia
Capital	Bogotá
Language	Spanish for the majority of the population; indigenous languages for a small minority; and English in San Andrés and Providencia
Population	36 million
Land Area	440,831 square miles (1,141,752 square km)
Departments	Antioquia, Atlántico, Bolívar, Boyacá, Caldas, Caquetá, Cauca, César, Chocó, Córdoba, Cundinamarca, Huila, La Guajira, Magdalena, Meta, Nariño, Norte de Santander, Quindío, Risaralda, Santander, Sucre, Tolima, Valle del Cauca
Highest Point	Cristóbal Colón (18,947 feet/5,775 m)
Major Rivers	Amazon, Atrato, Magdalena, Orinoco, Sinú
Longest River	Magdalena River
Main Religion	Roman Catholicism
Current President	Andrés Pastrana Arango (elected in 1998)
Currency	Colombian Peso (1,885 pesos = U.S. $1 in 2000)

Opposite: American tourists discover the beauty and magnificence of the Amazon River.

Glossary

ajiaco santafereño (ah-hee-AH-koh sahn-tah-fay-RAYN-yoh): a soup made from avocados, chicken, corn, and capers.

altitude: height above sea level.

arepas (ah-REE-pahs): cornbread.

chivas (CHEE-vahs): old-fashioned buses made of wood that are still used in rural areas.

coalition: a government made up of representatives from two or more political parties.

compadrazgo (kohm-pah-DRAHZ-goh): the Colombian social institution of godparenting.

compadres (kohm-PAH-drays): godparents.

conservatives: a Colombian political party that supported the idea of a strong central government.

dictatorship: a government ruled by a leader who has absolute power.

empanadas (aym-pah-NAH-dahs): snack pastries stuffed with meat and vegetables.

equator: an imaginary line around Earth that is an equal distance from both the North and South Poles.

filigree: delicate, lacelike ornamental designs made with gold or silver wire.

guerilla: related to soldiers who fight to change the existing political order.

indigenous peoples: groups of humans who originated in the place where they currently live.

inferior: low in quality.

La Violencia (lah vee-oh-LAYN-see-ah): the period of violent civil war (1948–1958) between Colombia's two main political parties.

liberals: a Colombian political party that supported the idea of federalism, or a weak central government.

literacy: the ability to read and write.

molas (MOH-lahs): decorated textile panels made by Cuna Indians.

privileged: having an advantage that most other people do not have.

repressed: put down.

rumba (ROOM-bah): a party that includes music, food, and dancing.

telenovela (tay-lay-noh-VAY-lah): a television soap opera.

temperate: neither extremely hot nor extremely cold.

More Books to Read

Botero: New Works on Canvas.
Fernando Botero
(Rizzoli Bookstore)

Colombia. Enchantment of the World
series. Marion Morrison
(Children's Press)

Colombia. Major World Nations series.
Tricia Haynes (Chelsea House)

*Colombia: The Gateway to South
America.* Lois Markham
(Benchmark Books)

Colombia from the Air.
Benjamin Villegas Jimenez
(St. Martin's Press)

*The Conquerors of the New Kingdom
of Granada.* Jose Ignacio
Avellaneda Navas (University
of New Mexico Press)

Culture and Customs of Colombia.
Raymond L. Williams
(Greenwood Publishing)

The Taste of Colombia. Benjamin
Villegas (St. Martin's Press)

Videos

Central and South America Box Set.
(IVN Entertainment)

*Lonely Planet Travel Survival Kit:
Colombia.* (Lonely Planet)

*Our Musical Heritage: Music of Latin
America.* (Hollywood Select Video)

*Travel the World by Train: South
America.* (Pioneer Video)

Web Sites

lcweb2.loc.gov/frd/cs/cotoc.html

www.odci.gov/cia/publications/
factbook/co.html

www.colostate.edu/Orgs/LASO/

www.lonelyplanet.com.au/dest/sam/
col.htm

Due to the dynamic nature of the Internet, some web sites stay current longer than others. To find additional web sites about Colombia, use a reliable search engine and enter one or more of the following keywords: *Amazon, Andes, Bogotá, Simón Bolívar, Fernando Botero, Colombian coffee, criollos, South America.*

Index

Afro-Colombians 21
agriculture 18
Amazon rain forest 9
animals 9
architecture 30
art 30, 31

beaches 37
beauty pageants 35
Bogotá 6, 7, 10, 13, 15, 16, 37, 41
Bolívar, Simón 10, 11, 12, 13
Botero, Fernando 31

Christmas 39
climate 8
Columbus, Christopher 5, 10
compadrazgo 23
conservatives 12
constitution 12, 16
crafts 33
criollos 21
culture 30, 32

de Paula Santander, Francisco 11, 15
de Quesada, Gonzalo Jiménez 10, 15
Drug Wars 14

economic class 20, 21
economy 18
education 24, 25, 26
emeralds 19
ethnic groups 21
exports 18

family 20, 22, 23, 35, 37
festivals 32, 38

government 13, 14, 16–17, 24, 25, 26
guerilla groups 14

health care 25, 26
Holy Week 38

independence 5, 10, 11, 29, 39
Independence Day 39
Indians 5, 20, 21, 30, 33
indigenous peoples 10, 29, 30, 32, 33

jewelry 30, 33

La Violencia 14
liberals 12, 15
literature 29

marriage 22, 26

mestizos 21
mining 19
mulattoes 21
music 32

New Granada 10, 15

Pinilla, Gustavo Rojas 13
population 7, 20, 21

rain forests 8, 9, 25
religion 20, 26, 27, 38
Roman Catholics 26, 27, 38

soccer 36
South America 5, 6, 11, 12, 28, 34
Spain 5, 10, 15
Spaniards 10, 11, 28, 30, 37
Spanish alphabet 28
Spanish conquest 10, 30
sports 36, 37

telenovela 34, 35

violence 13, 14, 27

water sports 37
whites 21